Strings

Wendy Lynch

Heinemann
LIBRARY

www.heinemann.co.uk/library
Visit our website to find out more information about **Heinemann Library** books.

To order:
 Phone ++44 (0)1865 888066
 Send a fax to ++44 (0)1865 314091
 Visit the Heinemann Bookshop at www.heinemann.co.uk/library to browse our catalogue and order online.

First published in Great Britain by Heinemann Library, Halley Court, Jordan Hill, Oxford
OX2 8EJ, a division of Reed Educational and Professional Publishing Ltd. Heinemann
is a registered trademark of Reed Educational & Professional Publishing Ltd.

OXFORD MELBOURNE AUCKLAND JOHANNESBURG BLANTYRE
GABORONE IBADAN PORTSMOUTH NH (USA) CHICAGO

© Reed Educational and Professional Publishing Ltd 2001
The moral right of the proprietor has been asserted.

Designed by Visual Image
Illustration by Jane Watkins
Originated by Dot Gradations
Printed and bound in South China

ISBN 0 431 12902 9

05 04 03 02 01
10 9 8 7 6 5 4 3 2 1

British Library Cataloguing in Publication Data

Lynch, Wendy
   Strings. – (Musical instruments)
   1. Stringed instruments – Juvenile literature
   I. Title
   787

Acknowledgements

The publishers would like to thank the following for permission to reproduce photographs: Associated Press p25,
Bubbles (Jennie Woodcock) p19, Gareth Boden pp11, 24, 28, 29, Greg Evans p20, John Walmsley p18, Photodisc pp6,
7, 10, 16, 17, Pictor pp4, 5, 9, Picture Colour Library Ltd p21, Redferns (Ebet Roberts) p26, Retna Ltd (Steve Jennings)
p27, Robert Harding pp15, 22, 23, Superstock p8, The Stock Market p13, Trevor Clifford p14.

Cover photograph reproduced with permission of Photodisc.

Every effort has been made to contact copyright holders of any material reproduced in this book.
Any omissions will be rectified in subsequent printings if notice is given to the Publisher.

Any words appearing in the text in bold, **like this**, are explained in the Glossary.

Contents

Making music together

There are many musical instruments in the world. Each instrument makes a different sound. We can make music together by playing these instruments in an **orchestra**.

Bands and orchestras are made up of different groups of instruments. One of these groups is called the string family. You can see many stringed instruments in this orchestra.

What are stringed instruments?

These are all stringed instruments.
They have strings stretched over them.
When the strings are played they
vibrate to make a sound.

sitar

harp

**electric
guitar**

You play some stringed instruments with a bow. A bow is a stick with horsehair or nylon stretched between the ends. You play others with a **plectrum** made of wood or plastic.

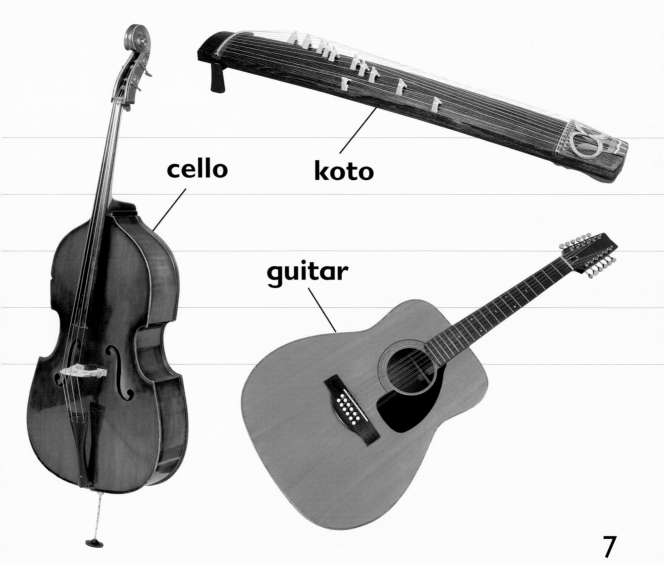

cello

koto

guitar

The violin

The violin is a popular stringed instrument. Many children learn to play the violin when they are young. You may learn to play on a small violin so that your fingers can reach across the strings.

You can learn to play the violin in school with a teacher. You can play the violin on your own. This is called playing **solo**.

Making a noise

The violin has four strings. It has a **curved** body and you play it with a bow. You move the bow across the strings to make a sound.

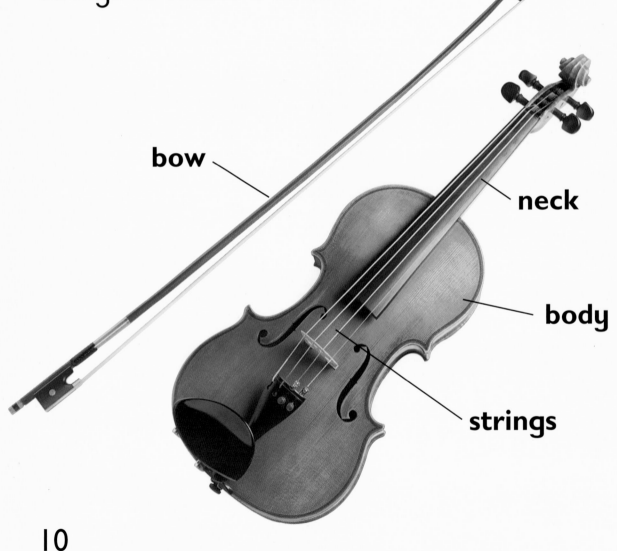

bow

neck

body

strings

You rub rosin into the part of the bow that touches the strings. Rosin helps the bow grip the string. Rosin is sticky stuff that comes from a tree.

How the sound is made

The body of the violin is **hollow**. We call it a sound box. When you move the bow across the strings, you make the strings **vibrate** from side to side.

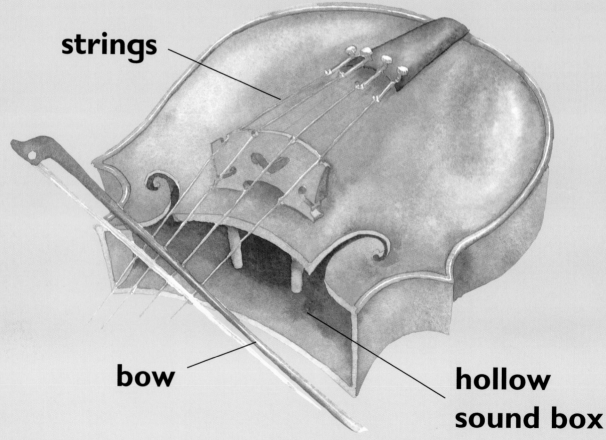

strings

bow

hollow
sound box

This movement of the strings makes
the air in the sound box vibrate. When
air vibrates, it makes a sound. You can
press your fingers against the strings
to change the sound.

Types of strings

The viola looks like the violin but it is slightly bigger. It also has a different **pitch** because the sound box is bigger than in the violin.

violin

viola

The cello is much larger than the violin. It also sounds much lower. To play, you use a bow and sit down and hold the cello between your knees.

Guitars

The guitar is a stringed instrument. You **strum** the guitar with your fingers or you can pluck it with a **plectrum**. To change the sound you press your fingers on the strings on the neck of the guitar.

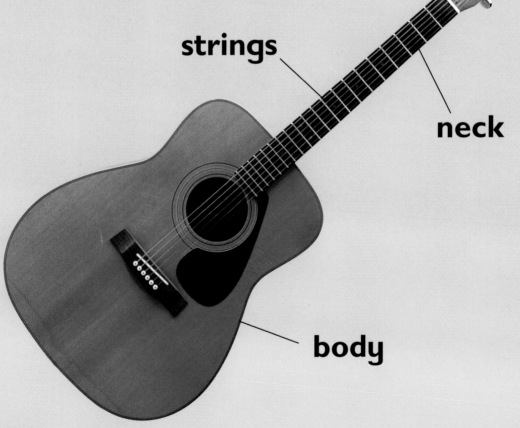

strings

neck

body

There are many different types of guitar. You can hear the steel guitar in **blues** and **folk music**. In **pop music**, you can hear the electric and bass guitar.

electric guitar

steel guitar

String concert

You may hear stringed instruments in a concert in school. In a string **quartet**, you can hear the cello, two violins and a viola.

Your teacher may play the guitar in school. These children are learning to sing a new song. Their teacher is **accompanying** them on the guitar.

The wider family

The harp is a **curved** instrument with 48 strings. The harpist sits and **plucks** the strings from both sides of the harp. Sometimes the strings are different colours. This helps the harpist find the notes.

You play the zither on a table or on your lap. On one side of the zither are five strings. This is where you play the **melody**.

Around the world

You can find stringed instruments all over the world. The sitar is from India. You **pluck** the strings with a wire **plectrum**. The sitar has two sets of strings, one on top of the other.

The koto is an old musical instrument from Japan. Women often play the koto. They sit on the ground to play it. One end of the koto rests on their lap, the other end rests on the ground.

Famous musicians and composers

Nigel Kennedy is a well-known violin player. This is a CD of him playing *The Four Seasons* by Vivaldi. Vivaldi **composed** a lot of music for the violin.

Sarah Chang began to play the violin when she was four years old. When she was five, she played in her first **public** concert.

Music now

Today you can hear stringed instruments in **jazz**, **rock** and Irish **folk music**. These people are playing Irish folk music. When you listen, it is easy to hear the violin.

You can hear people play electric guitars in rock and **pop music** today. You can also hear electric violins. You hear the sound from an electric guitar or violin through a loudspeaker.

Sound activity

You can make your own guitar. You need an empty tissue box, four rubber bands and a pencil. Wide rubber bands make a low sound, thin ones make a high sound.

Stretch the four rubber bands over the box from end to end. This is the sound box. Place the pencil under the rubber bands next to the hole. **Pluck** your guitar!

Thinking about strings

You can find the answers to all of these questions in this book.

1. What is rosin? How do you use it?

2. What is a **plectrum**?

3. Which instruments play in a string **quartet**?

4. From which country is the sitar?

Glossary

accompanying to go with

blues old style of slow, sad music from America

composed music that has been written

curved bent around

folk music old, traditional style of music from a place or country

hollow empty inside

jazz old style of music from America that is often made up as it is played

melody tune
You say *mella-dee*

orchestra large group of musicians who play their musical instruments together
You say *ork-es-tra*

pitch the highness or lowness of a sound or musical note

plectrum small piece of wood or plastic used to pluck the strings of some stringed instruments

pluck pull

pop music music of the last fifty years. A lot of people like this music.

public open to all or lots of people

quartet group of four musicians or piece of music for four players
You say *kwoor-tet*

rock music kind of pop music with a strong beat

solo song or piece of music for one person

strum to pull fingers down over the strings of an instrument

vibrate move up and down or from side to side very quickly

31

Index

A
accompaniment 19

B
bands 5
bass guitar 17
blues 17
bow 7, 10, 11, 12,
   15

C
cello 15, 18
Chang, Sarah 25
composers 24
concerts 18, 25

E
electric guitar 27
electric violin 27

F
folk music 17, 26

G
guitar 16–17, 19,
   27, 28–9

H
harp 20
horsehair 7

J
jazz 26

K
Kennedy, Nigel 24
koto 23

M
melody 21
musicians 24, 25

O
orchestras 4, 5

P
pitch 14
plectrum 7, 16, 22
plucking 16, 20, 22,
   29
pop music 17, 27

R
rock music 26, 27
rosin 11

S
sitar 22
solo playing 9
sound box 12, 13,
   14, 29

steel guitar 17
string quartet 18
strings 6, 10, 13, 16,
   20, 21, 22
strumming 16

V
vibration 6, 12, 13
viola 14, 18
violin 8–13, 18, 24,
   25, 26, 27
Vivaldi, Antonio 24

Z
zither 21

HFL version

Titles in the *Musical Instuments* series include:

Hardback   0 431 12900 2

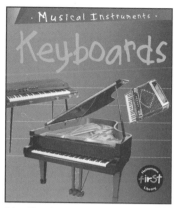

Hardback   0 431 12904 5

Hardback   0 431 12903 7

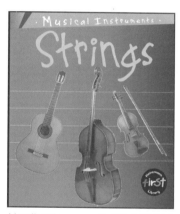

Hardback   0 431 12902 9

Hardback   0 431 12901 0

Find out about the other titles in this series on our website www.heinemann.co.uk/library